William Dallas Chesterman

The James River Tourist

A brief account of historical localities on James river, and sketches of

Richmond, Norfolk, and Portsmouth

William Dallas Chesterman

The James River Tourist

A brief account of historical localities on James river, and sketches of Richmond, Norfolk, and Portsmouth

ISBN/EAN: 9783337193324

Printed in Europe, USA, Canada, Australia, Japan

Cover: Foto ©Andreas Hilbeck / pixelio.de

More available books at **www.hansebooks.com**

WASHINGTON MONUMENT.

Corner-stone laid 22d February, 1850. Equestrian Statue unveiled 22d February, 1858. Total cost, $259,913.

Sixth Edition—Revised and enlarged every year.

THE JAMES RIVER TOURIST

A BRIEF ACCOUNT

—OF—

HISTORICAL LOCALITIES

—ON—

JAMES RIVER,

AND SKETCHES OF

Richmond, Norfolk and Portsmouth.

EDITED BY W. D. CHESTERMAN.

PUBLISHED BY LUCIEN B. TATUM,
Vice President Virginia Steamboat Company,
RICHMOND, VIRGINIA.

RICHMOND:
EVERETT WADDEY, PRINTER.
1889.

ST. JOHN'S CHURCH, RICHMOND,

Built about 1740. The oldest legible inscription on a tombstone is of date 1751. Rev. Miles Selden ("Parson Selden") was the Minister in Colonial times, and its first Rector.

☞ These Leading Hotels of Virginia are under one management. Having been connected by a Covered Suspension Bridge, thoroughly renovated and heated throughout by steam, can now offer most comfortable

and home-like accommodations for Six Hundred Guests. Rooms can be secured by telegraph or letter. $2.50, $3.00 and $4.00 per day.

J. L. CARRINGTON, Proprietor.

THE JAMES RIVER TOURIST.

Preface or Finis.—These lines will welcome the coming or speed the parting reader.

The book begins with Richmond and describes the points of greatest interest as the steamer moves on down the river. The reader who starts from Norfolk to Richmond, therefore needs to make "the last first," and begin at the end of the book. There will be no difficulty in fixing upon the localities mentioned if such person but remember to look to the *left* when the book points him to the *right* or *vice versa*.

> " The land was beautiful ;
> Fair rose the spires, and gay the buildings were,
> And rich the plains, like dreams of blessed isles."

The Locality of the City of Richmond was visited by Captains Newport and John Smith in 1607, the year of the settlement at Jamestown, and thirteen years prior to the landing of the Pilgrim Fathers on Plymouth Rock. In 1609 Captain Francis West and one hundred and twenty men were sent here from Jamestown "to settle," it was said, but they were little more than troops on an outpost, and their sufferings from hunger and Indian

NEWPORT NEWS,

NEAR OLD POINT COMFORT, VA.

❖ THE ❖

Hotel Warwick,

A Family Hotel of Superior Excellence

FOR THE ACCOMMODATION OF

WINTER and SUMMER VISITORS.

— × —

For terms, Illustrated Pamphlet, etc., address C. B. ORCUTT, Washington Building, No. 1 Broadway, New York, or

J. R. SWINERTON, Manager,

Hotel Warwick, Newport News, Va

(10)

depredations were great. For very many years the actual settlers were few in number. In 1737 Colonel William Byrd, of Westover, caused the town to be laid off into streets and lots on land belonging to him, and in 1742 it was duly incorporated by law. The seat of government was transferred from Williamsburg to Richmond by act of Assembly May, 1779.

The Colonial and Revolutionary history of Richmond is interesting; but it was as the Capital of the Confederate States, and as such the most prominent point of attack and defense in the late war, that its great celebrity was obtained.

The city is built upon many hills, and is remarkable for healthfulness; the streets, with few exceptions, intersect at right angles, and the residences are handsome and attractive. The tobacco trade, iron establishments and flouring mills, employ a large number of men and much capital. The shipments of tobacco, coal, flour, and products of field and forest generally, are considerable. There are regular lines of Steamers to Norfolk and all points on James river, (this line—the Virginia Steamboat Company), and to New York, Philadelphia and Baltimore. The seven railways centering in the city stretch out in nearly every direction. Petersburg is reached by rail in an hour, Washington in four hours, and New York in eleven. Population of Richmond and suburbs, 100,000.

Places at Richmond worth Visiting.—The Capitol Square is a lovely little park of sixteen acres, in

NATIONAL
BANK OF VIRGINIA,

Corner Main and Eleventh Street,

RICHMOND, VA.

— × —

UNITED STATES,

State and City Depository.

— × —

E. O. NOLTING,   J. W. LOCKWOOD,
President.   Cashier.

the heart of the city. In the midst of it stands the Capitol building or State House, the corner-stone of which was laid August 18th, 1785. The model was the Maison Caree of Nismes, France, selected for the State by Jefferson; but afterward somewhat altered. The marble statue of Washington, made by the great French Sculptor, Houdon, from casts taken from the PERSON of the FATHER OF HIS COUNTRY, is in the Rotunda.* The sessions of the Confederate Congress were held in this building. In 1870 the floor of the Supreme Court room, in the Capitol building, broke through, killing sixty-five persons and wounding about two hundred more. The State Library contains an extensive gallery of portraits of historical personages, nearly forty thousand volumes, and many curious relics. From the platform on the roof of the Capitol the very best view of the city and surrounding country can be obtained. In the Capitol grounds is the Washington Monument, the finest monumental pile and grandest group of statuary in America. It was designed by Crawford. The work left undone at his death was completed by Rogers. The figure of Washington on horseback is surrounded by statues of Jefferson, Henry, Marshall, Nelson, Mason and Lewis. Allegorical bronzes occupy the lower pediments. In this square are also the statues of Henry Clay, by Hart, and Stonewall Jackson, by the great English sculptor, Foley, now

---

*Col. Sherwin McRae has written, and the State has published, a valuable history of this statue, demonstrating that it is the most perfect likeness of Washington in existence.

Bay Line Steamers.

THE POPULAR, DIRECT AND MOST DELIGHTFUL

Tourist's · Guide

BETWEEN

New York, Philadelphia and Baltimore, and Old Point Comfort and Norfolk, and Principal Southern and Southwestern Cities.

— × —

Direct connection made at Old Point Comfort With Chesapeake and Ohio Railway, and at Norfolk and Portsmouth with Seaboard and Roanoke R. R., Norfolk and Western R. R., Norfolk Southern R. R., and Virginia Steamboat Company, for all points in Atlantic Coast States.

— × —

PALACE STEAMERS. UNSURPASSED CUISINE UNDISTURBED NIGHT'S REST. SURE CONNECTIONS.

— × —

D. J. HILL, Superintendent,   E. BROWN, G. T. A.,
Baltimore.   Baltimore.

H. V. TOMPKINS,
G. P. A., 287 Broadway. New York.

deceased, both presented to Virginia—the first by his countrywomen, the other by English admirers of the famous Confederate soldier. The Gubernatorial Mansion is within the enclosure of the square.

The other buildings in the city most interesting to visitors are : St. John's Church,* built about 1745, where Patrick Henry in 1775 made his speech, using the memorable words : " *Give me liberty or give me death ;*" the Monumental Church, marking the site of the old Richmond Theatre, destroyed by fire December 26th, 1811, (in which perished one hundred and twenty persons, including the Governor of the State, George W. Smith, and others of distinction ;) St. Paul's Episcopal church, where President Jefferson Davis was worshiping Sunday, April 2nd, 1865, when notified by General R. E. Lee of the breaking of the lines near Petersburg ; the Custom House, used by the Confederates as Treasury Department, and for offices of the President ; the Central School Building, formerly the residence of Hon. Jefferson Davis, and as such, "The White House" of the Confederacy ; the Old Stone House, on Main street, near Twentieth, which has some Revolutionary history ; the residence of General R. E. Lee, and the house of Chief-Justice Marshall, northwest corner of Ninth and Marshall streets.

Other places worth visiting are : the Tredegar Iron Works, which was the great cannon manufactory of the

---

*Its first pastor, and the first Episcopal minister in Richmond, was Rev. Miles Selden, familiarly called " Parson Selden."

CLAREMONT, VA.

J. FRANK

MANCHA'S

COLONIZING

AGENCY.

CLAREMONT, VA.

Confederacy; the Gallego and Haxall Flouring Mills, among the largest in the world; the tobacco factories, where the singing of the negro hands while manipulating the leaf is very entertaining; the Tobacco and Corn Exchanges, where samples of those staples are daily exposed for sale; and the studio of the sculptor, E. V. Valentine, 809 east Leigh street. The Libby and Belle Isle are of interest as former military prisons, Castle Thunder having been recently destroyed by fire.

The finest public buildings are the Custom House and Post-Office, the Almshouse, the Medical College and Y. M. C. A. The City Hall was pulled down several years ago to make room for a handsome new granite building which is now under construction. The handsome new Academy of Music has just been erected, and new Masonic Temple commenced.

At Oakwood Cemetery 17,000 Confederates are buried. A handsome monument has been raised over them. At Hollywood are the graves of 12,000 more. A granite pyramid ninety feet high has been erected in their memory by the ladies of Virginia. The graves of Presidents Monroe and Tyler, and Generals A. P. Hill, George E. Pickett, J. E. B. Stuart, and H. A. Wise, Commodore Matthew F. Maury, the journalist, Thomas Ritchie, (known as the "father of the Democratic party,") John M. Daniel, war editor of the "*Examiner*," the poet, John R. Thompson, and many other celebrities, are also there. Upon the northern limits of the city, at the terminus of Third street, are the Shockoe Hill and

STOVES, TINWARE

AND HOUSE-FURNISHING GOODS.

Hot Air Furnaces and Fire-Place Heaters.

L. W. GLAZEBROOK,

PLUMBING TINNING,

—— AND ——

GAS AND STEAM FITTING.

—— × ——

GAS FIXTURES

—— AND ——

SLATE MANTELS.

—— × ——

Orders Promptly attended to and Estimates Furnished upon Application.

—— × ——

No. 726 E. MAIN STREET,

RICHMOND, VA.

(18)

Jewish Cemeteries. In the former are buried Chief-Justice Marshall, John Hampden Pleasants, and many others of distinction.

A fine view of Belle Isle, Manchester and Richmond may be had from Hollywood. Just across the canal from that Cemetery is the Pump-House. The fashionable drive is to the New Reservoir Park and Soldiers' Home on the west of the city. The city's water is pumped from the river into two reservoirs northwest of Hollywood.

Monroe Park is near the western, and Marshall Park, (Libby Hill,) and Chimborazo Park, near the eastern end of the city. From both of the latter a fine river view may be had. A carriage may be taken and within a few hours' ride from the city several battle-fields and National cemeteries visited. In and about the city some 60,000 or 70,000 soldiers of the contending armies are buried. The Electric City Railway of Richmond is the longest in the world.

Manchester.—Opposite to Richmond, on the south bank of the James, is Manchester, (also a very old settlement,) a flourishing manufacturing city, containing about 10,000 inhabitants.

Two bridges for vehicles and foot passengers, and three for railroad cars, connect it with Richmond. A Street Car Railway connects Manchester and Richmond by the Free Bridge. A large number of the citizens are employed in cotton and flouring mills, granite works, and brick manufactories.

JNO. S. HARWOOD.   WM. F. HARWOOD.   R. H. HARWOOD.

HARWOOD BROS. & CO.

WHOLESALE DEALERS IN

OILS, GREASE
and GASOLINES,

11th and Cary Streets,

RICHMOND, VA.

---×---

White Lucent Premium Safety Oil, 160°, sole proprietors. Eureka Bright Machine and Spindle Oils. Mecca Engine and Excelsior Car Oils. Cylinder Oils

OFFICE, 1101, 2, 3, & 5, CARY ST.

Warehouse and Grease Works, 9th and Arch Sts.

THE LIBBY PRISON.

This building, erected as a store-house, was used during the war as a prison for Federal officers. In February, 1864, 109 of the inmates escaped by getting into the cellar, cutting through the wall, (opposite that bearing the sign), and tunneling outward into an old stable. About 60 were recaptured

DUNLOP DECORTICATED

Patent Family Flour.

FIRST PREMIUM AT VA. EXPOSITION.

— × —

JAMES RIVER FALLS FAMILY,

FIRST PREMIUM AT VA. EXPOSITION.

Superior for Family use to Spring Wheat and Western Brands.

— × —

ALL OTHER GRADES OF ROLLER FLOUR.

— × —

THE BEST NEW PROCESS

CORN MEAL,

—— AND ——

BRAN, BROWN STUFF,

—— AND ——

SHIP STUFF.

FOR SALE BY

DUNLOP & McCANCE,

MILLING AND MANUFACTURING COMPANY,

RICHMOND, VA.

The people are industrious and thrifty, and the city, like Richmond, is steadily growing in wealth and importance. Especially those interested in industrial enterprises will find a visit to Manchester profitable.

The Tourist.—The visitor leaving Richmond by the Virginia Steamboat Company's elegantly furnished and commodious steamer "Ariel," Captain Deyo, for any of the River landings, or for Old Point and Norfolk direct, and for all northern cities by its connections, at once enters into a country rich with historical associations.

It is the object of this work to point out to the traveler some of the famed localities and to refresh his memory with a few incidents of their history. The colonial records are crowded with details of the early settlements on the James. Revolutionary history abounds in facts relating to the river country. The literature of the last war is largely devoted to a recital of the operations of the armies upon these banks. From these and many other sources we gather these fragments, leaving untouched material sufficient for many volumes of history and romance.

The James River.—The Indians called the river Powhatan or King's river. The English under Newport and Smith, who entered it in 1607, gave it the name of James, in honor of their sovereign, King James I. Newport and Smith explored the river to the falls at Richmond in 1607, Smith describes it as follows:

"The mouth of this river is neare three myles in breadth, yet doe the shoules force the Channel so neare

YORK RIVER LINE.

DELIGHTFUL DAILY ROUTE

(SUNDAYS EXCEPTED.)

VIA CHESAPEAKE BAY.

ONLY **$2.00** BETWEEN

RICHMOND  BALTIMORE.

INVIGORATING SEA BREEZES,

INVITING MEALS,

COMMODIOUS STATE ROOMS.

For General Information apply to

G. F. NEEDHAM,
  G. P. A., York River Line,
    Light St., Baltimore, Md.

C. W. CHEARS,
  Ass't G. P. A., R. & D. R. R.,
    Richmond, Va.

the land that a *Sarce will overshoot it at point Blanche. It is navigable 150 myles. It falleth from Rockes farre west, in a country inhabited by a nation they call Monacans. But where it cometh into our discovery it is Powhatan. In the farthest place, [now Richmond,] that was diligently observed, are falles, rockes, shoules, &c., which make it past navigation any higher. Thence in the running downward the river is enriched with many goodly brookes, which are maintained by an infinite number of small rundles and pleasant springs, that disperse themselves for the best service, as do the veins of a man's body."

The entire length of James river from its source in Pendleton, W. Va., to its efflux in Chesapeake Bay, "is about 360 miles, but following its meanders, it is probable that the stream flows not much, if any less, than 500 miles." At several points, such as Dutch Gap, Curl's Neck and Jones' Neck, the river winds so much that its course is horse-shoe shaped, and vessels separated by several miles of river travel are only a short distance from each other by air line.

It is navigable from Richmond to the sea for vessels drawing sixteen feet.

Powhatan.—The brick building with trees about it, standing on the elevated ground on the left shore, and seen just after leaving this Company's wharf, was unquestionably the site of one of the residences of Powhatan, the great Indian potentate, who ruled over

---
*Species of falcon.

HOTEL

Twelfth Street Opposite Capitol Park,

RICHMOND, VA.

— × —

APPOINTMENTS FIRST CLASS.

— × —

Rates, $2.00, $2.50 and $3.00 per day.

— × —

First-Class Coaches meet all Trains and Steamboats.

— × —

CHARLES B. DODSON, Proprietor,

Connected with American Hotel for 12 years.

several tribes of Eastern Virginia in the early days of English settlement. Captain John Smith, condemned to death by this Powhatan, was saved by the entreaties of Pocahontas, the chieftain's daughter. This occurrence was at Werowicomico, on York river, near Shirley, in Gloucester county, Powhatan's chief place of residence. A boulder of about a ton in weight, bearing the traces of rude carvings, is pointed out at Powhatan as the tomb of King Powhatan, though it is now contended that he was not buried there.

Powhatan was seated by Joseph Mayo in 1725. His brother, Major William Mayo, surveyor, &c., laid off the cities of Richmond and Petersburg.

Whitby.—On the right bank of the James, where the new framed building is seen—was settled as early as 1620, thirteen years after Jamestown. An ancient record refers to it in a boundary line "As a place called Whitby, owned by Goode." Goode was an Englishman from Whitby, on the northeast coast of England.

James River Jetties.—The dykes and wing dams in the river, seen at and below Powhatan, are somewhat after the order of Ead's Mississippi River Jetties, and are intended to contract and deepen the stream. In this vicinity the United States Monitor Fleet is anchored.

Warwick.—A little over four miles from Richmond, on the high ground on the right (Chesterfield) bank, about where the old chimney stands, is the site of the former town of Warwick. Previous to the Revolution, and when the bars and rocks had not been removed to

(ESTABLISHED 1829.)

JULIEN BINFORD,

Successor to W. D. BLAIR & CO.

DEALER IN

FANCY GROCERIES,

Teas, Wines, and Liquors,

AND MANUFACTURERS' AGENT FOR

KEY WEST AND OTHER FINE CIGARS,

1202. E. MAIN STREET,

RICHMOND, VA.

—— × ——

Proprietor of the Celebrated "B-Select," "Glenwood," "Montrose" and "Alpha" Whiskeys; also Harvest Whiskey in Great Variety.

—— × ——

I have made a chemical examination of the "**Montrose**" Whiskey, the sample having been collected by me from many barrels, and find that it contains no impurities or adulterations. As a bevarage or medicinal agent it is entitled to full confidence.

WM. H. TAYLOR, M. D.,

Richmond, Va., February 26, 1885.   State Chemist.

—— × ——

I have analyzed the Whiskey known under the head of "**B-Select**," controlled by **Messrs. WALTER D. BLAIR & CO.**, Richmond, Va., and find it free from Fusil Oil and other impurities, and recommend its use for medicinal and family purposes.

J. B. McCAW, M. D.,

Late Professor of Chemistry, Medical College of Virginia.

admit of navigation to Richmond, this was a shipping point, and was a place of more importance than Richmond. Traces of the old wharves are yet to be seen at low tide. The town was burnt by Benedict Arnold's command of British troops in the Revolutionary war.

The poet, Edgar A. Poe, when quite a young man, for a wager, swam against a rising tide from a point near where the Ariel's wharf now is, to Warwick, and walked back to Richmond. The fact was attested by witnesses of it.

Confederate Pontoon Bridge.—Near the water-guage on the Warwick side, and at an opposite point on the other bank, are to be seen abutments of the old Confederate Pontoon Bridge, built of canal boats and schooners during the Seven Day's Battles in 1862.

Half a mile below the bridge was the first line of obstructions in the river, intended to stop Federal vessels should they pass Drewry's Bluff. There was a narrow and circuitous passage-way left open, through which vessels going to and from Drewry's Bluff could with proper caution pass.

Ampthill.—The dark brick house on the right, nearly surrounded by trees, and at considerable distance from the river, was the residence of Col. Archibald Cary, a prominent Revolutionary patriot. The bricks were brought from Europe, it is claimed. Wilton, across the river from Falling Creek, is another relic of antiquity.

Falling Creek.—This stream enters the James between Ampthill and Drewry's Bluff. On the banks

McADAMS & BERRY,

Leading Clothiers and Hatters,

1001 Main Street, corner Tenth,

RICHMOND, VA.

W. H. BRAUER,

BUTCHER

STALL No. 26 FIRST MARKET,

RICHMOND, VA.

— × —

DEALER IN PRIME FRESH MEATS.

— × —

MARKETING DELIVERED FREE.

of it, and about half a mile from the river shore, was erected the first iron furnace in the colony. In 1622, the date of the general massacre of colonists, Col. Berkeley and twenty of the operatives were killed by the Indians. Mr. R. A. Brock, Secretary Virginia Historical Society, whose historical researches and writings have been of great value, thinks that a furnace was again worked here by Col. Wm. Byrd, the *first* of the name, in 1690. It is believed that the first furnaces were operated with bog or surface ore, which abounds in the locality. Col. Archibald Cary, who conducted the furnace in 1760, and some time afterwards, obtained his ore from the Potomac. Col. Cary's works were burnt by Tarlton during the Revolution.

The abutment piles of a Confederate military bridge can be seen near the mouth of Falling Creek. At the time of the evacuation of Richmond a considerable portion of Gen. Lee's army from the north of the James crossed this bridge on their way to Petersburg and Appomattox C. H.

***Drewry's Bluff, or Fort Darling.**—On the right side of the river, where the bank rises high, is Drewry's Bluff. The steamer reaches it half an hour after leaving Richmond. When the fortifications were incomplete here, in May, 1862, the Federal fleet (Monitor, Galena, Aroostook, Naugutuck, Port Royal and others), were ordered to proceed to Richmond and "shell the city

---
* It was called Fort Darling by the Federals and Drewry's Bluff by the Confederates.

C. E. JONES. THOMAS POINDEXTER. THOS. N. JONES.

JONES, POINDEXTER & CO.

WHOLESALE GROCERS,

AND DEALERS IN

TOBACCO AND CIGARS,

No. 1112 E. CARY STREET,

RICHMOND, VIRGINIA.

PURCELL, LADD & CO.

—WHOLESALE—

DRUGGISTS

RICHMOND, VA.

—×—

Agents for the following Waters of the Virginia Springs, and other Celebrated Mineral Waters of this Country and Europe:

Wolf Trap Lithia, White Sulphur, Rockbridge Alum, Alleghany, Healing, Buffalo Lithia, Blue Ridge, Wallawhatoola Alum.

(32)

into a surrender." They were not aware that the river had been obstructed at the Bluff by the Confederates sinking steamers and canal boats loaded with stone. The Federal fleet, however, never reached the obstructions. After a hot fight and considerable Federal loss the fleet retired. Thirteen shots were put through the Galena. Subsequently the Bluff was made a very Gibraltar for strength.

General B. F. Butler made an attack on the line to the right of Drewry's Bluff in May, 1864, and succeeded in forcing his way to the Richmond and Petersburg railroad, but was soon compelled to retire before the Confederates to Bermuda Hundred.* Several of the buildings used for officers' quarters and many of the earthworks are still standing.

Wilton Creek enters the river from the left bank (north side) after Drewry's Bluff is passed. Off the mouth of this creek the Federal gun-boats anchored to attack Drewry's Bluff.

Chaffin's Bluff.—The bluff below Wilton Creek is Chaffin's. It was very strongly fortified by the Confederates after the battle with gun-boats at Drewry's Bluff. Earthworks still visible.

The Grave-Yard Landing—Fort Harrison.—In the grave-yard near this wharf, (on the left bank), there was a Confederate signal station for some

---

*In conformity with the Code of Martial Law each hundred (colonists) were subjected to the control of the Captain.—*Campbell*. Hence Bermuda Hundred, Flowery Hundred, &c. The first name of the plantation was Bermudas; afterward called Bermuda Hundred.

P. J. CREW & CO.

DIXIE SOAP WORKS

113, 115 AND 117 SEVENTEENTH ST.,
RICHMOND, VA.

—×—

Manufacture the Standard Grades of Laundry Soaps, which we offer to the trade at lowest Market Price.

HABLISTON & BRO.
NEW AND ARTISTIC
FURNITURE
PARLOR SUITS.

Hall, Library, and Sitting Room Pieces

OF EVERY DESCRIPTION.

Bed-Room Furniture in Suits or Single Pieces,
SPRING BEDS, MATTRESSES, ETC.

Our Assortment will please you in Quality, Quantity and Price.

905 MAIN ST., RICHMOND, VA.

"While lingering rivers in meanders glide,
They scatter verdant life on either side."
—*Blackmore.*

VIEW OF JAMES RIVER BELOW THE CITY.

Old Dominion Steamers

—— FOR ——

LEAVE

RICHMOND via James River every
TUESDAY and FRIDAY
at 5 P. M.

FARE—CABIN,

Including Meals and Stateroom Berth.

To New York, - - - - -	$ 9 00
To New York and return, good for 30 days, -	14 00

STEERAGE.

With Subsistence, - - - -	$6 00
Without Subsistence, - - - -	5 00

Passengers can leave Richmond via Chesapeake and Ohio Railway, and via Petersburg and the Norfolk and Western Railway every Monday, Tuesday, Wednesday, Thursday, and Saturday, connecting at Norfolk with Ship for New York the same evening. Fare, straight, $10; Excurrsion, $14, good for 15 days.

The Steamer "**ARIEL**" from Richmond Wednesday mornings will connect at Norfolk with Ships leaving same evening.

Steamers leave New York for Richmond, via James River, every Wednesday and Saturday at 3 P. M. from Pier 26 North River.

Tickets for sale at Chesapeake and Ohio and Richmond and Petersburg Depots, A. W. Garber's, 1000 Main Street, Company's Office, 1301 Main Street, and aboard Ships.

GEO. W. ALLEN & CO.,

Agents.

months. Looking back up the river and to the right of Chaffin's you have a fine view of Fort Harrison.

On the 29th of September, 1864, two corps of Butler's army surprised and wrested Fort Harrison from the small Confederate garrison. They then attempted to carry Fort Gilmer, adjacent to Fort Harrison, but were repulsed with great slaughter. The attacking party was mostly composed of negroes. On 30th September General Lee, with two Confederate divisions, endeavored to retake Fort Harrison, but in vain.

Devil's Reach.—The stretch of water in front of the settlement on the right bank is known as Devil's Reach. The Confederate flag-of-truce steamer Shultz, having been down the river and delivered a number of Federal prisoners for exchange, near here ran upon a Confederate torpedo and was destroyed.

Three or four men were killed. Her commander, Captain D. J. Hill, was thrown overboard, but was happily saved to grace his present position as Superintendent of the Bay Line steamers between Baltimore and Norfolk.

Where the shores approach each other closest the river is 450 feet wide, and in the channel sixty-five feet deep.

Signal Hill.—The high ground seen from Cox's wharf, looking back up the river, is Signal Hill. It was at first a Confederate signal station, and later a Federal fort. A path leads up the hill from the river's edge.

Confederate Batteries.—The redoubts on the right side of the river were a portion of the Confederate

G. W. WARREN,   W. R. QUARLES,
Late Real Estate Broker.   Late Cashier Planters National Bank.

WARREN & QUARLES,

BANKERS AND BROKERS,

1117 MAIN ST., RICHMOND, VA.

STOCKS, BONDS, GOVERNMENT, STATE, CITY AND OTHER SECURITIES

Bought and Sold on Commission.

—×—

Loans Negotiated.   Correspondence Solicited.

RICHMOND TRANSFER COMPANY,

—AND—

General Railroad and Steamship Ticket Office,

1000 EAST MAIN STREET.

THROUGH TICKETS TO ALL POINTS

NORTH, SOUTH, EAST, AND WEST,

AND EUROPE.

Sleeping and Parlor Car Accommodations secured.
Passengers and Baggage called for at Hotels and Private Residences for all trains and steamers leaving the city.
Baggage checked to destination.
Pleasure carriages with intelligent drivers for hire at reasonable rates.
Information cheerfully given by addressing

A. W. GARBER, 1000 East Main Street.

(38)

line, which extended from below Drewry's Bluff to Howlett's farm and thence to Petersburg.

Around Farrar's Island.—Steamers now go through Dutch Gap instead of rounding Farrar's Island, or "the cut off." Travelers thus save almost half hour, but miss sight of the Howlett House Batteries—a strong Confederate position—and Osbornes', the latter a shipping point for coal brought down by rail from the Chesterfield Pits.

Dutch Gap Canal.—This interesting point is an hour's ride by steamer from Richmond. The river here makes a long sweep around the narrow neck of land known as Farrar's Island.

Ralphe Hamor, sometime Secretary of the Colony, in his notes printed in 1615, says of this place:

"Sir Thomas Gates and party left Jamestown in the year 1611, with 350 men, such as he himself made choice of, and in a day and a half landed at a place where he purposed to seate and builde, where he had not bin ten daies before he had very strongly impaled seven English acres of ground for a towne, which, in honor of the noble Prince Henrie," * * "he called by the name of Henrico." * *

"There is in this towne three streets of well framed houses, a hansom church, and a foundation of a more stately one laid of brick, in length a hundred foote, and fifty foote wide, besides store-houses, watch-houses, and such like; there are also on the verge of the river five block houses, with centinelles for the town's security."

Locomotives for every variety of service.

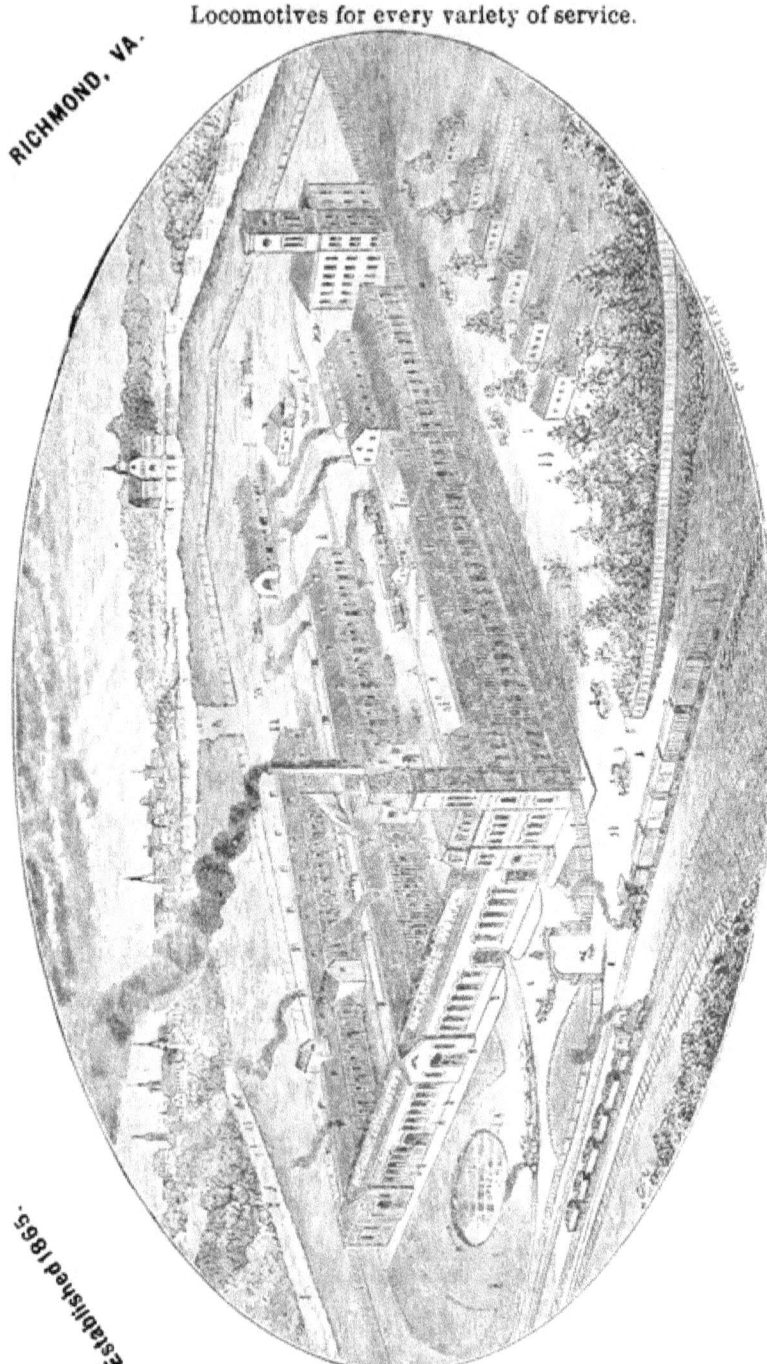

RICHMOND, VA.

RICHMOND LOCOMOTIVE & MACHINE WORKS.

Established 1865.

Catalogues, Estimates, and Specifications on application.

The town was abandoned after a few years.

Bishop Meade, in his "Old Churches and Families of Virginia," says:

"It has also been called Dutch Gap, because there are indubitable marks of the commencement of a channel by the first Dutch settlers across its narrow neck, by which the water might be let through and seven miles of travel thus saved. The channel was opened about half way across—that is, about sixty yards and then abandoned. The city laid off here was called Henricopolis, or the City of Henry. It was afterward, in common use, contracted to Henrico."

Standing on an elevation on the island, one may here see what appears to be four rivers, such are the meanders of the James.

General B. F. Butler. in 1864, undertook to cut the canal through the narrow neck, with the object of allowing the Federal gun-boats to evade the heavy Confederate batteries on Howlett's Bluff, opposite the other end of the island. The Confederates daily shelled the working parties, and many men were killed in the ditch. Butler had, however, nearly completed the canal to a depth of five or six feet when, he says, he received an intimation from the naval authorities to cease work, as they feared, from a formidable demonstration the Confederate gunboats had then but recently made, that the latter would come through the canal and interfere with the Federal operations.

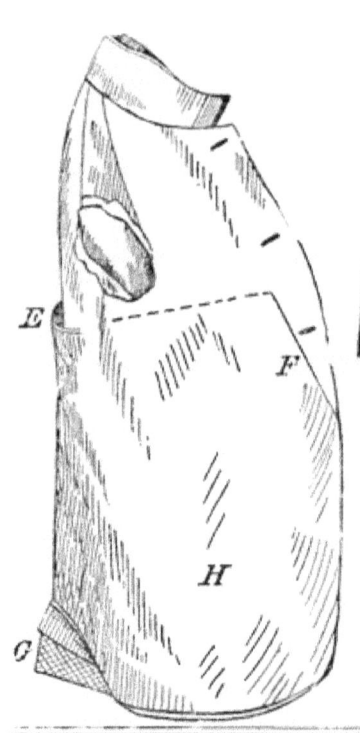

Hunting Outfits.

A. SAKS & CO.,

1003 Main St.,

OPPOSITE P. O.

RICHMOND, VA.

HENRY BUCKER'S

STEAM BOTTLING

WORKS.

Agent for GEO. EHRET'S New York Lager Beer. GEO. EHRET'S New York and SCHLITZ Milwaukee Export Beers a Specialty.

2120 AND 2122 EAST MAIN STREET,

RICHMOND, VA.

In 1871 and 1879, by expenditures of considerable money by the United States Government and city of Richmond, the canal was deepened and widened and made navigable. Its length is four hundred and eighty-one feet, width about two hundred and fifty, depth of channel-way sixteen feet at low tide. In March, 1879, while a party of men were engaged on the north bank in the work of widening the canal, the premature explosion of a can of nitro-glycerine killed M. C. Heggarty, Elias G. Hall, and Alexander Brown, and wounded others.

Varina, or Aiken's Landing.—In the first settlement here "Master Rolfe, sometime Secretary of the Colony," resided after he had married Pocahontas, daughter of Powhatan, and celebrated as the saver of Captain John Smith's life. The name Varina was given because the tobacco produced here was similar to that produced at Varina, in Spain. The county seat of Henrico was for a long time here. It was removed from here to Richmond The British under Benedict Arnold burnt the settlement during the revolution.

For a considerable period of the late war Varina was neutral ground, and here many thousand prisoners were exchanged. On this account the place is best known. In the large red-brick house, near the wharf, (on the left shore,) the commissioners of exchange of the two armies often held their meetings.

Deep Bottom.—Collection of fishermen's huts on the left. There were several severe engagements in this vicinity during the war. In 1864 one of Butler's gun-

E. J. BOSHER.   C. G. BOSHER.

R. H. BOSHER'S SONS.

MANUFACTURERS OF FIRST CLASS

CARRIAGES, BUGGIES, WAGONS, &C.

A large stock of vehicles of every description kept always on hand. Repairing done in the best manner and at reasonable rates. Doctors' Buggies a Specialty.

No. 15 SOUTH NINTH STREET,

RICHMOND, VA.

E. B. TAYLOR & CO.

HOUSEHOLD GOODS,

Glassware,   Clocks and

Tinware,   Lamps.

FANCY GOODS,

WHOLESALE and RETAIL.

1011 MAIN STREET, Opposite Post-Office,

RICHMOND, VA.

(44)

boats, while attempting to pass this point, was destroyed by a Confederate torpedo, and forty-five men killed. An unusual ripple in the stream marks the place where she went down and her wreck yet lies.

Curl's Neck.—From Deep Bottom to City Point the course of the river is something like the letter S, with Curl's Neck on the left, and Bermuda on the right.

Turkey Bend.—Here McClellan took refuge under cover of his gun-boats after the Seven Day's Battle around Richmond. Turkey Island Plantation (on the left) was the home of General Pickett, who led the Virginia Division in their celebrated charge at Gettysburg. The residence was destroyed by fire from the gun-boats. There was formerly an island in the river here much frequented by wild turkeys, and from it the place took its name. The island long since disappeared. A buoy marks the place where it is believed to have been.

Malvern Hill.—This place—the high ground on the left bank—is best seen as the steamer approaches Turkey Island wharf. Here McClellan, in July, 1862, after the bloody battles around Richmond, made his last stand and repulsed the attack of a portion of the Confederate army under General McGruder. He held his ground at Malvern Hill for several days, and then retreated to Harrison's Landing.

Presque Isle.—The large new framed barn to the right, is on the Presque Isle Plantation. From this vicinity the chimneys of the Shirley house, distant eight or nine miles by the windings of the river, but not a

JOHN BOWERS,
No. 7. (Iron Block) Governor St.,
RICHMOND, VA.

BRASS FIRE SETS.

Chandeliers, Fancy Colored Globes, Brass Fenders, and And Irons, Iron and Terra Cotta Urns.

Stoves, Furnaces, Ranges, Marbleized Slate Mantles, Tile Hearths, Fronts and Grates

REFRIGERATORS AND OIL STOVES A SPECIALTY.
SEND FOR CIRCULAR.

— THE POPULAR —

Dry Goods and Carpet House,

LEVY & DAVIS,

1017 & 1019 MAIN STREET.

ONE PRICE ONLY.

Agents for the Whitney Baby Carriages.   A full Stock of Toys at all times.

fourth of the distance by direct line, may be plainly seen. In Colonial days Presque Isle was known as Bermuda Nether Hundred.

Shirley.—This fine old homestead occupies an eligible site on the high ground on the left bank. A glimpse of it, through the trees, may be caught after the wharf is passed The house of brick was built in 1642, it is said, but certainly prior to 1700, and is yet in an excellent state of preservation.

Annie Carter, wife of Light Horse Harry Lee of Revolutionary fame, and mother of General R. E. Lee, was born here.

Bermuda Hundred.—The settlement on the right (between the James and Appomattox), is known as Bermuda Hundred. It is in Chesterfield county, and is the eastern terminus of the Brighthope Railroad. The Indian massacre here in 1622, "was great."

General B. F. Butler having, in 1864, advanced to Chester Station, on the Richmond and Petersburg Railroad, and being compelled to retire, found a place of refuge on this neck of land. General Grant said that Butler's condition (though he had 25,000 or 30,000 men) was as helpless as though he were corked up in a bottle. Hence "Butler bottled up."

City Point.—This place, in Prince George county, is two and one-half hours run from Richmond by steamer. The Appomattox here joins the James, rounding the point of land upon which the village is built.

RICHMOND STRAIGHT CUT
❋ No. 1 ❋
CIGARETTES

☛ Cigarette Smokers who are willing to pay a little more for Cigarettes than the price charged for the ordinary trade Cigarettes will find the

RICHMOND STRAIGHT CUT No. 1 Superior to all others.

They are made from the brightest, most delicately flavored, and highest cost gold leaf grown in Virginia, and are absolutely without adulteration or drugs. We use the Genuine French Rice Paper, of our own direct importation, which is made especially for us, water marked with the name of the brand—

RICHMOND STRAIGHT CUT No. I,

on each Cigarette, without which none are genuine. Base imitations of this brand have been put on sale, and Cigarette smokers are cautioned that this is the **Old** and **Original** brand, and to observe that each package or box of Richmond Straight Cut Cigarettes bears the signature of **ALLEN & GINTER**, Manufacturers, Richmond, Va.

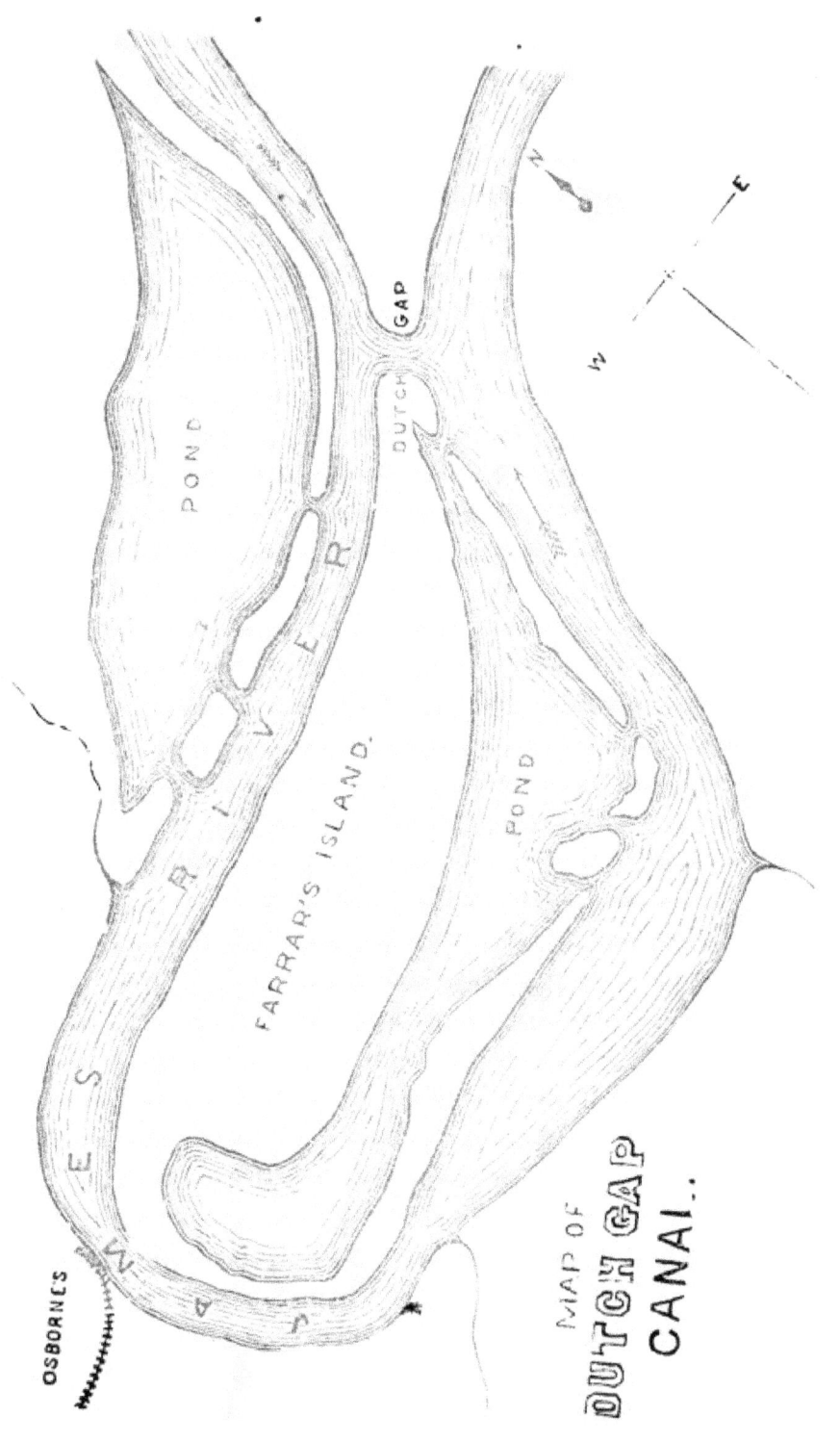

SAVAGE AND HOLMS,

FACTORY 324 SOUTH SIXTH STREET,

MANUFACTURERS OF FINE

HARD-WOOD

WORK.

—×—

MANTLES, BAR FIXTURES,

OFFICE, STORE AND LIBRARY FITTINGS,

ETC.

—×—

RICHMOND, VA.

The Appomattox is navigable to the historic city of Petersburg, and a railroad of nine miles length connects that city with the Point. Much of the shipping of Petersburg is done here.

General Grant had his headquarters at City Point during the siege of Petersburg.

President Lincoln was here on a visit when Richmond was evacuated, and went hence to Richmond, and upon his return to Washington was assassinated.

Scenery, Crops, &c.—As the boat leaves City Point a fine view of river scenery may be had. The James river lands, both above and below this point, yield richly of corn, oats, wheat, peanuts, truck, &c.

In the early days of Virginia history, the great crop on James river was tobacco. Little of it is now produced in this section; other crops which pay better and require less care, being preferred. The great tobacco producing region of Virginia now is on both sides of the James above the falls, in the Piedmont country, and in the counties of Southside Virginia.

The waters of the James yield liberal supplies of fish. In the marshes, in the early weeks of autum, thousands of sora are killed and sent to the cities for sale. There are fine marshes at Aiken's, Curl's Neck, Turkey Island, Brandon, and Westover.

In season, partridges may be killed in the fields, and wild ducks and other water fowl on the banks of the stream. Many sportsmen come here, some in their fine steam yachts from the North, as guests of the planters, to exercise their skill.

R. B. CHAFFIN & CO.,
REAL ESTATE AGENTS and AUCTIONEERS,
No. 1 N. Tenth Street, Richmond, Va.

Purchasers introduced to owners. Land shown to buyers free. Large quantity of City Property, and 600 Farms and Mills for sale and exchange. Property in City and Country sold privately or by auction. Rents collected and advances made thereon. Money loaned on Real Estate in the City or Country. Deeds written and acknowledgments taken. Write for Free Real Estate Journal. The largest advertisers of Real Estate in America, except Western Railroads. Reference by permission, First National Bank.

On the right, three miles below City Point, is Jordan's Point Light-house.

Berkeley.—A few miles below City Point, on the left shore, is Berkeley or Harrison's Landing. Berkeley is an old Colonial residence. President (Tippecanoe) Harrison was born here in 1773. The house is of English brick, in good repair. After the battle of Malvern Hill, McClellan retreated to this point and fortified himself. From Coggin's Point, on the opposite shore, the Confederates, on one occasion, shelled McClellan's shipping in the river, doing it great damage.

From "Camp near Harrison's Landing," on July 4th, 1862, General McClellan issued his "congratulory order" to his troops, saying, "We have succeeded in *changing our base* of operations by a flank movement," &c., and his army was soon afterwards embarked for Acquia Creek.

In 1864 General Wade Hampton, with a command of Confederate cavalry, starting from Petersburg, made a circuit around the Union lines and swept down to Sycamore church, near Coggin's Point, where he seized, and then drove back to the Confederate lines, 2,500 beef cattle, 200 mules, and 300 prisoners.

John Tyler, the tenth President of the United States, and the sixth from Virginia, was born in Charles City county, in 1790, about five miles below Berkeley. Four miles lower down on the river was his residence. His grave is in Hollywood Cemetery, Richmond.

JOHN L. WILLIAMS.   JNO. SKELTON WILLIAMS.

—×—

John L. Williams & Son,

Bankers and

Brokers,

No. 1014 MAIN STREET,

RICHMOND, VA.

—×—

P. O. BOX 225.

—×—

Transact a general Banking and Brokerage Business. Deal in Southern Investment Securities. Negotiate Railroad and Municipal Loans.

(54)

The Massacre of 1622.—The Colonial Records contain a list of those massacred by the Indians on this river in 1622. The places (many of which may be readily identified) and numbers are as follows: "At Berkeley's Plantation, seated at Falling Creeke, some 66 miles from James Cittie, 27; At Master Thomas Sheffield's Plantation, some three miles from Falling Creeke, 15; At Henrico Iland, about two miles from Henrico Cittie, 17; At Apomattucke River, at Master Abram Pierce, his Plantation, some five miles off the Colledge people,* 4 ; At Charles Cittie, and about the precincts of Capt. Smith's Company, 5; At other Plantations next adjoining, 8; At Mr. Wm. Farrar's House, 10; At Berkeley Hundred, some five miles from Charles Cittie, 17; At Westover, about a mile from Berkeley Hundred, 33; At Flowerdieu Hundred, Sir George Yeardley's Plantation, 6; At the other side of the River, opposite Flowerdieu Hundred, 7; At Mr. Swinehowe's, 7; At Mr. Wm. Bikar's House, 5; At Weyanoack, of Sir George Yeardley, his people, 21; At Powle Brooke, 12; At Southampton Hundred, 5; At Martin Brandon's, 7; At Capt. Spilman's House, 2; At Ensigne Spence, his House, 5; Persons slaine at Martin's

---

**The College Land.*—"In 1619 Sir Edwin Sandys moved and obtained that ten thousand acres of land should be laid off for the University at Henrico, a place formerly resolved on for that purpose. This was intended as well for the college for the education of the Indians as to lay the foundation of a Seminary of learning for the English."—*Stith.* "On the northerly side of James River, from the falls down to Henrico, containing ten miles in length, are the public lands reserved and laid out, whereof are ten thousand for the University lands, 3000 are for the Company's lands, with other lands belonging to the College."—*McDonald Papers.*

EVERETT WADDEY,

MANUFACTURING STATIONER,

BOOKBINDER

AND PRINTER,

No. 1112 MAIN ST.,

RICHMOND, VIRGINIA

—×—

AGENT FOR THE

SCHLICHT & FIELD

Labor-Saving Office Devices,

METAL ROLLER SHELVING, DOCUMENT FILES, &C.

The only house in the State carrying in Stock a complete line of Legal Blanks for the use of Attorneys, Clerk of Courts Commissioners, Magistrates, &c.

(56)

Hundred, some seavan miles from James Cittie, 79; At Mr. Thomas Pierce, his House, over against Mulberry Island, 6; At Mr. Edward Bennet's Plantation. 53; At Master Walter's House, 5. Total, 347."

Westover.—This fine residence of English brick (on the left) has long been celebrated in Virginia History. The name of Westover appears as far back as 1623. Here was for many years the county seat of Charles City county, which then occupied both sides of the River. The Plantation was settled by Sir John Paulett, from whom it passed into the hands of Theodrick Bland, and then to William Byrd, the father of Colonel William Byrd, the founder of Richmond, and one of the most celebrated men of his day. The present house was built by Colonel Byrd in 1737. On the 4th of January, 1781, Benedict Arnold, in command of a force of British troops, landed here, marched on Richmond, captured the place, and burnt the public stores. Arnold was twice here whilst ravaging the James river country. Lord Cornwallis, moving from Petersburg to the Peninsula, prior to the battle of Yorktown, with the bulk of his army, crossed the river at Westover, using the British fleet, and probably also Swinyard's ferry, which was then in operation on "the King's highway," some miles below the Westover house.

General Pope and other Union generals had their headquarters here during the late war. For generations Westover was the homestead of the Selden's, a famous old Virginia family, but is now owned by Major A. H. Drewry.

T. L. ALFRIEND,

No. 1203 Main St., Richmond, Va.

WASHINGTON
LIFE INSURANCE CO.
OF NEW YORK.

ASSETS, - - $10,000,000.

29 YEARS IN EXISTENCE.

The only Company whose dividends are Premium-Paying and Policy-Protecting for their full amount, without notice to the insured and without medical re-examination.

ALSO AGENT IN

Fire, Marine and Steam Boiler Insurance

———FOR THE———

Phœnix Assurance Company, of London; Germania Fire Insurance Company, of New York; Home Insurance Company, of New York; Boston Marine Insurance Company, of Boston, Mass.; American Steam-Boiler Insurance Company, of New York.

Capital represented, over $30,000,000. Deposited with State Treasurer, $155,000.

(58)

Wilcox's Landing--Fleur de Hundred.—
The narrow neck of land running into the river from the (right) shore opposite Wilcox's wharf, is Windmill Point—Fleur de Hundred plantation. In 1864 Grant, in his movement from Spotsylvania Courthouse to the front of Petersburg, laid a poontoon bridge across the river from Wilcox's wharf to Windmill Point, and another lower down the river at Fort Powhatan, and marched his army of 130,000 men over them in forty-eight hours.

Queen's Creek.—A short distance below Wilcox's this stream enters the James. Charles City Courthouse, a place famous in colonial, revolutionary, and more recent annals, is but a few miles from here.

Weyanoke.—This is a fine old colonial homestead (on left bank). The house is one mile from the wharf, and is only visible from the upper deck of the steamer. The house nearer is a modern structure. Weyanoke was the scene of a massacre of English settlers by the Indians

Fort Powhatan.—Below Weyanoke wharf and where the river narrows, is Weyanoke Point (on the left), and Fort Powhatan (on the right). On the left are are to be seen, at low tide particularly, the piles or stakes out from which Grant's poontoon bridge was laid.

Fort Powhatan was built during the revolutionary war by order of Baron Steuben. Col. Christ. Senf, who had been an Engineer in Frederick the Great's service, was the military constructor. The bricks were furnished by Col. Harrison, of Lower Brandon, and the earthwork done by negro slaves. A fleet of British vessels were

FOURQUREAN, PRICE & CO.,

429 E. Broad St., 206 & 208 N. Fifth St.,

RICHMOND, VA.

SHOPPING BY MAIL SAVES MONEY, TIME, AND TROUBLE.

Our Sample Department is in charge of a capable Salesman, whose pleasure will be to fill your orders with CARE and PROMPTITUDE. Order samples and make your selection from them. Estimates furnished for the Seasons outfit, in

UNDERWEAR, WALKING COSTUMES AND BRIDAL TROUSSEAU.

---×---

OUR STOCK Is always the Largest, Freshest, and Best in SILKS, VELVETS, PLUSHES, DOMESTICS, REX GOODS, CLOTHS AND CASSIMERES, NOTIONS, LACES AND EMBROIDERIES, DRESS GOODS, LINENS, &c.

---×---

Cloaks and Wraps of every Description, including Seal Skin and Astrachan of our own manufacture. Dress Trimmings, Fancy Worsteds and Fancy Wares. Agents for Butterick's Paper Patterns. Agents for Dr. Jæger's Sanitary Woolen Goods.

(60)

driven back here in 1781, but General Phillips landed below, and flanking, took it. The fort was armed and garrisoned in the war of 1812.

In the War of 1861-5 it was a strong Confederate position until the lines were drawn close around Richmond and Petersburg, when it fell into the hands of the Federals.

Upper Brandon.—About five miles from Fort Powhatan, and on the same (right) side of the river, is Upper Brandon, a large and fine old plantation.

Wilson's Wharf.—Two miles further on, on the left bank, is Wilson's Wharf, indentified with the movements of both armies in the late war. The water in the channel very near there, as appears from the United States Coast Survey, is ninety-five feet deep.

Lower Brandon.—This house, one of the oldest and best on James river, is concealed from view by the fine trees by which it is surrounded. It is the homestead of the Harrisons. Here is a gallery of portraits, including some collected by Colonel Byrd, and others added to them by the Harrisons.

Claremont.—Chipoak Creek enters James river (from the right) between Lower Brandon and Claremont.

Claremont, in Surry county, was the residence and and property of the late Major Wm. Allen. The estate embraced 13,000 acres of land, bounded on the north by James river and on the west by Chipoak creek. It has a water frontage of seven miles. This estate was bought in 1879 by J. Frank Mancha, of Delaware, who imme-

HOWARD SWINEFORD,

AGENT FOR THE

LARGEST LIFE

——AND——

Fire Insurance Companies

IN THE WORLD.

OFFICE, 1108 MAIN STREET,

RICHMOND, VA.

HE MUTUAL LIFE INSURANCE COMPANY, OF NEW YORK, with assets of over One Hundred and Twenty-Six Millions of Dollars, issues every form of Life and Endowment Policies, and returns all profits to its Policy-Holders, thereby making it the Cheapest and Best, as it is the Largest and Strongest, Company in the world. The New Distribution Policies are marvels of simplicity and fairness, which an experience of Forty-Six years has perfected.

The Fire Branch of this agency, backed by $60,000,000 of capital, furnishes Policies at current prices, and on application in person or by letter, of the following old and fire tried Companies:

THE ROYAL, OF LIVERPOOL.
THE IMPERIAL, OF LONDON. THE NORTHERN, OF LONDON. THE CONNECTICUT, OF HARTFORD.

Satisfactory Settlements. Prompt attention to business.

diately subdivided it into over two hundred farms, which he has since sold to northern and western settlers. Under this management a village has sprung up of about 100 houses, eight or ten stores, three hotels three factories, two churches, a school, &c. The village cannot be seen from the river on account of the high bluff and forest trees.

The village was incorporated in 1885, and has a Mayor and council. Mr. Mancha has lately extended his colony by a purchase of 8,000 acres more, which is also offered in small farms. The property has been divided into numerous small farms to be sold to settlers.

Claremont is the terminus of the Atlantic and Danville Railroad, which is being rapidly pushed to completion. This railroad has already reached Hicksford, 60 miles distant, and runs through a rich cotton, peanut and timber country. It is rapidly extending to Danville, Va.

Full particulars of this mammoth enterprise will be cheerfully sent on application by the founder, J. Frank Mancha, Claremont, Va.

Sandy Point.—This place is across the river from Claremont. It was settled by Colonel Phillip Lightfoot, ancestor of Lighthorse Harry Lee, and General R. E. Lee. Part of the old homestead is still standing. The present house was built about 1717, and is in good repair. There is fine snipe-shooting here.

Dancing Point—A Tradition.—The Promontory at the junction of the Chickahominy with the James, is Dancing Point.

THE
CONTINENTAL BREWING CO.

BREWERS OF

PURE ALE,

PORTER AND

LAGER BEER.

WE MAKE A SPECIALTY OF

BOTTLED GOODS,

DELIVERED IN ANY PART OF THE CITY.

RICHMOND DEPOT—Broad & Kinney Sts.

Phones: { 71 in the Day. { 76 at Night.

ROBERT HILL, Jr., Manager.

It derives its name from a tradition that was once current among sailors on the river. The property was owned by a man who may be, for this purpose, called Lightfoot. On the plantation there was a marsh which the owner was very desirous of cleaning up, and tradition says that the scheme was violently opposed by the devil. An interview between his Majesty and Lightfoot took place, during which it was agreed that a trial of dancing should be held to decide whether the marsh should be cleared up or not. The night was appointed and the spot chosen. At the hour the parties met, and commenced their exercises. Flaming torches and shooting stars rising from the swamp lighted the ground upon which the contest took place.

When morning broke the devil retired, and Lightfoot discovered that the spot formerly occupied by the swamp was a field, high and dry. Lights still float over the field at night, and on the ground where the dance took place no grass nor herb will grow. A bare spot of a hundred yards in extent still marks the scene of the strife. No freedman's foot crosses this spot after nightfall, and no fox seeks here his prey. That's what "they say."

The Chickahominy.—This river comes into the James at Dancing Point. It rises about fifteen miles northwest of Richmond. At about five miles of Richmond it is a small stream flowing through swampy lands, but towards the mouth it becomes navigable for steamers.

Captain John Smith, while endeavoring to discover the headwaters of the Chickahominy, was captured by the Indians, led about the country, between the James and Potomac, for several weeks as a prisoner, then carried before Powhatan, at his seat on Pamunky (now York river), called "Werowicomico," and condemned to death, but rescued by the tearful entreaties of Pocahontas. The Chickahominy was an important line in the military movements of 1862 and 1864. On or near its banks, but within hearing of Richmond, were fought the important battles of Mechanicsville, Ellerson's Mill, Gaines' Mill, Cold Harbor, Savage's Station, and Seven Pines, or Fair Oaks, and dozens of lesser engagements.

SMITH'S RESCUE BY POCAHONTAS.—Smith's General Historie, relating how the Captain, after a gallant defence, was captured by the Indians while exploring this stream, says that "having feasted him after the best barbarous manner they could, a long consultation was held, but the conclusion was, two great stones were brought before Powhatan. Then, as many as could, laid hands on him, dragged him to them, and thereon laid his head; and, being ready to beat out his brains, Pocahontas, the King's dearest daughter, when no entreaty could prevail, got his head in her arms, and laid her own upon his to save him from death. Whereat the Emperor was content he should live to make him hatchets, and her bells, beads, and copper; for they thought him as well [skilled] of all occupations as themselves. For the King himself will make his own robes, shoes, bows, pots; plant, hunt, or do anything so well as the rest. * * * Two days after Powhatan came to him and told him that he should go to Jamestown, to send him two great guns and a grindstone, for which he would give him the country of Capahowsick, and forever esteem him as his son Nantaquond. So to Jamestown, with twelve guides, Powhatan sent him. That night they quartered in the woods, he still expecting—as he had done all the time of imprisonment (six or seven weeks)—every hour to be put to one death or another, for all their feasting. But Almighty God, by his Divine Providence, had mollified the hearts of those stern barbarians with compassion. The next morning betimes they came to the fort, where Smith, having used the savages with what kindness he could, showed Rawhunt, Powhatan's trusty servant, two demi-culverins (cannon) and a millstone to carry Powhatan. They found them somewhat too heavy, but when they did see him discharge them, being loaded with stones, among the boughs of a great tree loaded with icicles, the ice and branches came so tumbling down that the poor savages ran away half dead with fear. But at last we regained some conference with them, and gave them such toys, and sent to Powhatan, his women and children, such presents as gave them in general full content."

Jamestown, or " James Cittie."—At Jamestown one comes upon the memorials of a long vanished past. Here was the first effectual settlement of English in America, and here was the first capital of the colony, and the palace of the Royal governors and council who, with mimic pride, emulated the grandeur and pageantry of Whitehall. The town, or "cittie," as it was fondly called, was laid off into several fair streets. Many of the houses were of considerable size and architectural pretension.

The tower of the church, seen on the left as the boat approaches the wharf, is the only vestige of the colonial buildings now standing.

From Jamestown Captain John Smith went on his exploring expeditions to the falls of the James, towards the headwaters of the Chickahominy, and up the Chesapeake.

In 1609, Smith having received a severe wound from an explosion of gunpowder, returned to England. The next year, the colonists greatly reduced by death and famine, abandoned Jamestown, "and one day re-embarked for England at noon. Near the mouth of the river, the next morning, they met Lord Delaware with three ships," bringing reinforcements and provisions, and with him they returned to Jamestown.

Two years later Pocahontas fell into the hands of the colonists under Captain Argall "When she was taken to Jamestown a message was sent to Powhatan that he must ransom her with certain men and articles, which he was accused of having taken. To this the Chieftian made no reply for three months. In the meantime John Rolfe had wooed the maiden and obtained her consent to marriage." She received Christian baptism under the

RUINS OF THE OLD CHURCH AT JAMESTOWN.

One mouldering tower, overgrown with ivy, shows
Where first Virginia's Capital arose,
And to the tourist's vision far withdrawn,
Stands like a sentry at the gates of dawn.
The church has perished—faint the lines and dim
Of those whose voices raised the choral hymn ;
Go read the record on the mossy stone,
'Tis brief and sad—oblivion claims its own.
Thompson's Virginia.

name of Rebecca, and for some time resided at Varina. She died in England, leaving one child. Some of the proudest Virginia families claim descent from her.

In 1619 the first legislative assembly in America met at Jamestowm.

About this time a considerable number of young women of humble birth, but "pure and incorrupt," were sent over here and sold to the planters as wives for an amount about equal to their passage money, the price being paid in the then currency of the colony, tobacco.

In 1620, a Dutch ship from Africa arriving at Jamestown, sold to the colonists twenty negro slaves. Thus was laid the foundation of negro slavery in America. The general massacre of settlers on and near the James, occurred March 20th, 1622. Three hundred and forty-seven persons were slain. The people of Jamestown, receiving a timely warning from a friendly Indian, were saved.

1676 Jamestown was burnt during the civil war between the patriot colonists under Bacon, and the Royal Governor Berkeley.

In 1698 the capital of the colony was transferred to Williamsburg, and Jamestown went into decay.

The old church, of which the entrance tower remains, was not the first erected in the town, but is, nevertheless, of great antiquity. It is surrounded by a graveyard, in which many of the colonists were buried. The inscriptions on the tomb-stones are but partly legible.

"It is difficult," says the author of the British Spy,

"to look at this venerable steeple, surrounded as it is with these awful proofs of the mortality of man, without exclaiming in the pathetic solemnity of Shakespeare:

> "The cloud-capped towers, the gorgeous palaces.
> The solemn temples, the great globe itself;
> Yea, all which it inherits, shall dissolve,
> And like this insubstantial pageant faded,
> Leave not a wreck behind."

The breastworks to the left of the church were erected by Major Allen, of Claremont, and were occupied by the Confederates until the evacuation of Norfolk and the Peninsula between the James and York rivers.

The house fronting the river was the original residence of Governor Berkeley.

The river below here, where it broadens widely, is called Cobham Bay.

Hog Island—Homeward P. O.—A few miles on from Jamestown we come abreast of Hog Island (point of land to the right). One of the settlements made soon after the landing at Jamestown was there. It is owned by E. E. Barney, Esq., formerly of Ohio, who has converted it into a large stock farm, and erected valuable improvements.

King's Mill Wharf—Williamsburg.—On the left shore, and nearly opposite Hog Island, is King's Mill Wharf. Williamsburg is four miles distant.

This city was the seat of the Colonial Government anterior to and for a short time during the Revolution. It was first settled in 1632. The venerable William and

Mary College, here founded in 1692, is the oldest educational establishment in the United States, except Harvard. An appeal for its relief has been urged before Congress, its losses by the war having been some $80,000. In the lawn fronting the college is the ancient statue of Lord Botetourt, the "popular Governor" of the colony.

PALACE OF LORD DUNMORE.—The remains of this regal domain of the last Royal Governors are still to be seen on the Main Street. It was accidentally burned by French soldiers soon after the surrender of Lord Cornwallis at Yorktown.

The OLD CAPITOL was also destroyed by fire 1832. Some of the arches, half concealed in the green sward, are yet to be seen. This was the celebrated "House of Burgesses," where Patrick Henry made that famous revolutionary speech, ending in the sentence, "*If this be treason, make the most of it!*"

The RALEIGH TAVERN, with its historical associations and its celebrated Apollo room, has also yielded to the ravages of fire, and not a vestige remains to connect the present with its eventful past.

The venerable Episcopal church, one of the oldest in Virginia, and the Magazine, or *Old Powder-Horn*, as it is familiarly called, still stand, relics of "ye olden tyme." The latter has long since been shorn of its glory, and is now utilized as a stable.

The city is very interesting to tourists, and is well worth visiting.

Yorktown, on York river, is twelve miles from Williamsburg. There Lord Cornwallis surrendered to Washington, virtually closing the war for American independence.

Mulberry Point.—Seven or eight miles from King's Mill Wharf, on the same shore, and where the river narrows, beyond Deep Water Light, is Mulberry Point.

Here the Jamestown refugees first saw Lord Delaware's fleet. Smith's History says: "At noone they fell from Jamestown to the isle of hogs, and the next morning to Mulberry Point, at which time they descried Lord Delaware's long boat, for God would not have the settlement so abandoned," &c.

Burwell's Bay.—A fine sheet of water. Here the river is five miles in width. The water is shallow except in the channel in which the boats run.

Between Mulberry Point and Newport News are the Point of Shoals Light and White Shoal Light. Warwick river enters the James from the left, and Pagan creek and Nansemond river from the right.

Part of Cornwallis' forces crossed here on the march to Yorktown in 1781.

Ferguson's Wharf is the next landing on the south side. It has a thriving railroad formerly run by bogies, but now by steam engines, and extends 13 miles. Large quantities of peanuts, lumber and merchandise are carried over this railroad.

Turner's Wharf is in sight from Ferguson's. It also has a railroad run by locomotives and does a similarly large business.

Newport News.—The point of land extending down into the water from the left is Newport News. Pig Point is on the opposite shore. Here is the mouth of James river and the opening into Hampton Roads. On a bright day the church spires at Norfolk, fourteen or fifteen miles distant, may be seen. Hampton and Old Point are also in view.

Newport News was fortified by the United States troops early in the war.

Off Newport News 8th of March, 1862, was fought the great naval battle between the United States vessels Congress, Cumberland, Minnesota and St. Lawrence, and the Confederate iron-clad ram Virginia (or Merrimac) and the steamers Patrick Henry and Jamestown, and two or three small gun-boats. The Virginia ran her sharp-pointed prow into the Cumberland (one of the very largest ships in the United States navy), and sunk her. She went down, carrying with her a great number of her officers and crew. When the tide is coming in or going out ripples are seen over the spot where her wreck yet lies. Any officer of the boat will point them out to you. The Congress was disabled, run ashore, surrendered, and was then burned by the Confederates. The Federal batteries at Newport News took some part in the fight.

The victory was a great one for the Confederates. It demonstrated that wooden vessels were powerless before iron-clads, and revolutionized naval architecture the world over.

The night after this battle the United States iron-clad Monitor arrived in Hampton Roads. Next day there was an indecisive fight between her and the Virginia.

A few months later the Monitor was lost at sea, off Cape Hatteras. The Merrimac was blown to pieces by the Confederates upon the evacuation of Norfolk.

The celebrated Confederate cruiser Florida, taken in the Port of Bahia, was brought into Hampton Roads and sunk near Newport News, pending the demand of the Brazilian authorities for her return to Bahia. The Brazilians claimed that in her capture the neutrality laws had been violated.

One of the finest hotels in the country has been erected here—"The Warwick"—which is much resorted to by tourists.

Hampton.—The town on the left is Hampton. Its site was visited by Captain John Smith in 1607.

Burk says: "The colonists, while engaged in seeking a fit place for the first settlement, met five of the natives, who invited them to their town, *Kecoughtan*, or *Kechotan*, where Hampton now stands. Here they were feasted with cakes made of Indian corn, and regaled with tobacco and a dance."

The locality was settled in 1610, by people from Jamestown.

There was a considerable battle near the settlement between the Indians and whites.

The town was attacked by the British in the war of the Revolution, and also in 1813, and on each occasion was valorously defended. On the first occasion successfully; on the second Admiral Cockburn's men got into the town and sacked it.

In 1862 it was burned by the inhabitants and General Magruder's Confederate troops.

In Hampton still stands the pretty little church of St. John, built somewhere between 1660 and 1667. This is, says Dr. W. P. Palmer, editor of the Calendar of Virginia State Papers, and a recognized authority in such matters, "One of the few church buildings the bricks of which were brought from England."

Near Hampton, in the civil war, was the great camp for refugee slaves—"contraband of war," as General B. F. Butler called them.

Hampton is a pleasant place to visit at all times. Many families from the cities spend their summers here. It commands a fine water view.

BARNES' HOTEL, located here, (J. J. Barnes, proprietor,) is pleasantly situated, has recently been completely refitted, and is a popular summer resort. The fare is excellent, and the proprietor and his assistants exert themselves to render the guests comfortable. There are billiard-rooms and bath-house attached to the hotel.

"When the fury of an Atlantic storm drives vessel after vessel into the secure anchorage of the Roads, until a whole fleet is gathered under the guns of Old Point Comfort; or when, on some bright, breezy morning, scores of white-winged oyster-boats put out from every safe nook of the shore, dotting the sparkling blue of the bay like snowy birds; or, better still, when the fading crimson glow of sunset makes the shore shadowy and indistinct, and the little flotilla comes tranquilly homeward to the slow dip of oars, and the weird, rich singing of the negro boatmen—then one gazes and listens, to confess that at last such scenes are hard to rival, and that this bit of coast need not fear the verdict of critics with whom still lingers the remembrance of Mediterranean skies or distant tropic seas." So says Mrs. M. F. Armstrong, in the interesting little book entitled "Hampton and its Students."

Hampton Institute.—The fine, large brick edifice, seen as we pass Hampton, is Virginia Hall, the main building of the Hampton Normal and Agricultural Institute, of which General S. C. Armstrong is principal. It was established in 1868, by donations from the Freedmen's Bureau and liberal Northern people, for the education of colored girls and boys.

In 1872 the General Assembly of Virginia assigned to the Institute one-third of the Land Script (worth $95,000) received for educational purposes from the United States Government. There are now at the Institute about three hundred students. Fifty or sixty of these are Indian boys and young men from the extreme western frontier. Thousands of people from the Hygeia Hotel visit the Institute.

The Indians are objects of special interest. The plantatation songs of the negro students are delightful to hear.

The boys receive military instruction at the hands of Captain Henry Rameyn, U. S. A. There are several work-shops for practical training; the idea being to fit the students for the earnest work of life.

Soldiers' Home.—The fine large building, with cupola, next seen as we approach Old Point, is the National Home for disabled Volunteer Soldiers, built and used before the war as a female college. Over seven hundred veterans now have a comfortable home here. Colonel P. T. Woodfin is in charge. The grounds are lovely, and are a favorite resort for pic-nic parties from Norfolk, Portsmouth, Hampton and Old Point.

Near to the Soldiers's Home is a National Cemetery. A fine monument stands as a memorial of the 6,000 men who there lie buried.

The Home, the Hampton Institute, and the town of Hampton may be easily and quickly reached from Old Point by boat or carriage.

Old Point Comfort—Fortress Monroe.—The name "Poynt Comfort" was given the neck of land lying between Chesapeake Bay and Hampton Roads, in 1607, by the first Colonists, "on account of the good channel and safe anchorage it afforded." It is called Old Point Comfort to distinguish it from New Point Comfort, near the mouth of the York river. Its advantages as a defensive position were at once seen by the settlers, and they built a fort here. A short time previous to the surrender of the British at Yorktown, Count De Grasse, the French Admiral, threw up some Fortifications at Point Comfort.

The present Fortress was commenced in 1819, and named in honor of President Monroe. It is the largest and strongest in this country. Its full armament is b tween four and five hundred guns. Fortress Monroe was the basis of operations for many of the movements against the Confederates in Virginia, North Carolina, and more Southern States.

Hon. Jefferson Davis was for a long time after the close of the war imprisoned here. The casemate which was his prison is shown to visitors.

Hygeia Hotel.—The Hygeia Hotel is situated upon the beach, near to the wharf, and within one hundred yards of the Fortress. It has accommodations for 1,000 guests, and has all modern improvements—gas and electric bells in every room, bath-rooms on each floor, elevator, etc. Ten or fifteen steamers land at the wharf each day, except Sunday, and there is quick communi cation by mail and telegraph with all parts of the world.

The best class of Northern people assemble here in winter, and of Southerners in the summer months.

From the great porticoes of the hotel Capes Henry and Charles light-houses (at the points where the Bay joins the Atlantic) may be seen day or night without a glass.

The beach at Old Point is beautiful. It is hard and smooth, and the shore declines into the water so gradu-

FIGHT OF THE MERRIMAC AND THE MONITOR.
From Butler's Pictorial History U. S.

Monitor to the left.

Merrimac to the right.

ally that bathers may secure any depth they may desire. The surf dashes almost up to the hotel steps—a great advantage—as the ladies can walk from the dressing-rooms in the hotel right out into the water. There is no undertow, and no dangerous current to excite fears of accident, while the water is almost as salty and strong as in mid ocean. The guests enjoy the bathing free from any restrictions except the conventional bathing-dress.

There are plenty of boats on hand to be hired to fishing parties, or for excursions to the Rip-Raps, Soldiers' Home, Hampton Institute, or town of Hampton.

There also several pretty carriage drives.

The parade ground within Fortress Monroe is delightfully shaded with live oaks. The famous Artillery School has its establishment within the Fortress, and the guard-mount and dress-parade, with the music of a fine band each morning and evening, give the visitors a pleasure rarely found at the seaside, or at any other resort.

The fare is excellent, as the hotel is within easy reach of the Norfolk, Richmond and Baltimore markets, and is in the midst of a great oyster and fish-producing country. The hotel is open all the year.

The climate during the year is unsurpassed for salubrity. The range of the thermometer here for the past ten years, as taken from the notes of the Meteorological Observatory, shows an average of 60°, 70°, 76° in summer; 70°, 59°, 46° in autumn; 45°, 44°, 42° in winter; 48° 52°, 63° in the spring months.

Rip Raps.—Going from Old Point to Norfolk, immediately after starting, you pass to the right of the Rip Raps—first called Fort Calhoun; afterwards Fort Wool.

"The channel which leads in from the Capes of Virginia to Hampton Roads," says Martin's Gazetteer, "is at Old Point Comfort reduced to a very narrow line. The shoal water, which, under the action of the sea, and reacted upon by the bar, is kept in an unremitting ripple, has given the name of Rip Raps."

Fort Calhoun—or the Rip Raps, as it is commonly called—was, in conjunction with Fortress Monroe, expected to completely bar the entrance of Hampton Roads to the shipping of the foreign enemy. It is built upon an island formed of stones brought from long distances at great cost. It has never been completed, and probably never will be, since it cannot be made effective as against iron-clads.

The extremity of land south of the Rip Raps is Willoughby's Point.

Sewell's Point.—The next prominent projection of the land from the left is Sewell's Point. The Confederates, strongly fortified here, had several sharp engagements with the United States gunboats in 1861 and 1862.

Craney Island.—This place (to the right, where the large brick buildings are seen,) is five mile from Norfolk. The Government powder magazines are located here.

In 1813 the British, under Admiral Cockburn, attacked the Virginia troops defending Craney Island, and were most signally defeated, and Norfolk and Portsmouth were thus saved.

Near here, upon the evacuation of Norfolk by the Confederates in 1862, the iron-clad Virginia (Merrimac) was blown up, her draft of water being too great to enable her to get to Richmond.

Fort Norfolk — Marine Hospital.— When about to enter the superb harbor of Norfolk and Portsmouth, we pass to the left of Fort Norfolk, and to the right of the Marine Hospital. The latter is in the midst of a grand natural park.

Norfolk.— As you steam into the harbor, Norfolk is to the left and Portsmouth to the right—the Elizabeth river dividing them. They are called the "Twin Sisters by the Sea." Observing the precept, "Emulation without envy," they are both increasing in population, wealth, and industrial and commercial importance. Here is a lovely climate. The Gulf Stream, which touches the Virginia shore, robs the atmosphere of its frostiness in winter, and the heats of summer are kindly tempered by the fresh breezes from the sea.

The colonists early foresaw the advantages of Norfolk as a seaport, and it was established as a town in 1705. Among its many objects of interest is "Old St. Paul's church," the mother church of Elizabeth-River Parish, the most ancient edifice in the city, built of imported brick in 1739. During the war of 1776 the British robbed the church, carrying the communion plate of silver, to Scotland. On the south corner may now be seen, half imbedded in the bricks, a small cannon ball, which was fired from the frigate Liverpool, of the British fleet, when the town was bombarded and destroyed. This church was about the only building that escaped destruction, and the people have refused to alter its exterior, permitting it to remain as a landmark of "old times."

People fond of good eating will especially be pleased with Norfolk and Portsmouth. The earliest vegetables and fruits reach these markets, and the finest oysters and fish here abound.

Norfolk has a population of 30,000, and is now the second cotton port in the United States. The Liverpool, Memphis and Norfolk Steamship Line dispatch steamers direct to Liverpool during the cotton season.

The operations of the great steam cotton presses (by which the bale of the planter is reduced to about one-third of its original size) are interesting to witness. Norfolk and Portsmouth ship immense quantities of truck, oysters and fish to the markets in Northern cities. Norfolk is the headquarters of the North Atlantic squadron, and the flag-ship, the old-fashioned but comfortable steam frigate Powhatan, spends most of her time in the harbor, adding to the pleasure and gaiety of the port by its fine band. The Receiving-ship Franklin has also a superior band, that discourses fine music. The numerous visits of our own and foreign men-of-war contribute much to the social life of Norfolk, which is proverbially agreeable and enjoyable.

The drives to Ocean View, Water-Works, Bowden's Ferry, etc., are very pleasant.

Norfolk has several first-class hotels.

Portsmouth.—Immediately opposite Norfolk (and connected therewith by a steam ferry) is the city of Portsmouth, established in 1752. In common with Norfolk it possesses one of the best harbors in the world, in which the vessels of our navy are generally lying at anchor. Its commodious water-front affords berths for the largest ships.

In the centre of the city, on one of its principal streets, the ladies have erected a monument of Southern granite to the Confederate dead of Portsmouth.

Here, in 1775, Dunmore, the Royal Governor, a fugitive from Williamsburg, erected his standard. In 1780 the traitor, Arnold, had his headquarters at Portsmouth.

The United States Navy-yard, one of the largest and best, is directly on the southern extremity of the city, about half a mile from its centre, in that portion called Gosport, where the General Government has built a large dry dock of Richmond granite, costing one million of dollars, and capable of admitting the largest ships. It is fitted up with all the latest modern machinery. Work done here, it is claimed, is superior to that of any other yard.

Population of Portsmouth by Census of 1880, 11,388.

Norfolk and Portsmouth are connected with the South and Southwest by railroad, and by first-class steamers with the chief seaboard cities of the country. Richmond is reached by James river by the Virginia Steamboat Company Tuesdays, Thursdays and Saturdays, leaving Norfolk at 6:30 A. M. New York is twenty-two hours distant by water. Philadelphia is eighteen hours distant; Clyde steamships leave Mondays, Wednesdays and Saturdays at 7 P. M. Baltimore, twelve hours : Bay Line steamers leave daily, except Sunday, at 6 P. M. Washington, twelve hours; Tuesdays, Thursdays and Saturdays, 4 P. M. Boston, forty-eight hours; Tuesdays and Fridays, 3 P. M. Providence, Wednesdays and Saturdays, 1 P. M.; also by Clyde Line, tri-weekly, and to Fall River. Old Point, about three-quarters of an hour by the Virginia Steamboat Company's fast steamer Ariel, is touched at both on inward and outward trip from Norfolk, during the summer season, and by other steamers; consequently passengers can reach that delightful summer and winter resort frequently during the day.

The locks of the Dismal Swamp canal are only five miles distant, and Lake Drummond about twenty.

. A line of steamers leave for points on both the Dismal Swamp and Albemarle and Chesapeake canals on alternate days—the latter on Mondays, Wednesdays and Fridays, at 6 A. M ; the former on Tuesdays, Thursdays and Saturdays, at same hour.

Berkeley.—This is a beautiful little village, situated at the head of the harbor of Norfolk and Portsmouth, between the two cities, and connected with them by a steam ferry. Many of the merchants have made their homes here, and it is rapidly growing in population and wealth.

A number of lumber and other mills are here doing a flourishing business.

Lake Drummond has a world-wide reputation, gained in part by the poem by Tom Moore (written by him while on a visit to Norfolk), entitled "The Lake of the Dismal Swamp."

It is based on a story told of a young man who lost his mind upon the death of the girl he loved, "and who, suddenly disappearing from his friends, was never afterwards heard of. As he had frequently said in his ravings that the girl was not dead, but gone to the Dismal Swamp, it is supposed that he wandered into that dreary wilderness, and had died of hunger, or been lost in some of its dreadful morasses." Moore makes the young man say:

> "They made her a grave too cold and damp,
>   For a soul so warm and true:
> And she is gone to the Lake of the Dismal Swamp,
> Where all night long by a fire-fly lamp,
>   She paddles her white canoe."
>
> "And her fire-fly lamp I soon shall see,
>   And her paddle I soon shall hear;
> Long and loving our life shall be,
> And I'll hide the maid in a cypress tree,
>   When the footstep of Death is near!"

Away to the Dismal Swamp he speeds—
  His path was rugged and sore ;
Through tangled juniper, beds of reeds,
Through many a fen, where the serpent feeds,
  And man never trod before.

And when on the earth he sunk to sleep,
  If slumber his eyelids knew,
He lay, where the deadly vine doth weep
Its venomous tear, and nightly steep
  The flesh with blistering dew!

And near him the she-wolf stir'd the brake,
  And the copper-snake breath'd in his ear,
Till he starting cried, from his dream awake,
"Oh! when shall I see the dusky lake,
  And the white canoe of my dear?"

He saw the Lake and a meteor bright
  Quick over its surface played—
"Welcome," he said, "my dear one's light,"
And the dim shore echoed for many a night
  The name of the death-cold maid!

Till he hollowed a boat of the birchen bark,
  Which carried him off from shore ;
For he followed the meteor spark—
The wind was high, and the clouds were dark,
  And the boat returned no more.

But oft from the Indian Hunter's camp
  This lover and maid so true
Are seen at the hour of midnight damp
To cross the lake by a fire-fly lamp,
  And paddle their white canoe.

Finis or Preface.—These lines will speed the parting or welcome the coming reader.

The book begins with Richmond and describes the points of greatest interest as the steamer moves on down the river. The reader who starts from Norfolk to Richmond, therefore needs to make "the last first," and begin at the end of the book. There will be no difficulty in fixing upon the localities mentioned if such person but remember to look to the *left* when the book points him to the *right*, or *vice versa*.

www.ingramcontent.com/pod-product-compliance
Lightning Source LLC
Chambersburg PA
CBHW020302090426
42735CB00009B/1182